Q
QUAIL

Sarah Hatton Knits
10 Simple Projects For Cosy Babies

First published in Great Britain in 2013 by
Quail Publishing
www.quailpublishing.co.uk

Second Edition Reprint - May 2013

An imprint of Daco Technology Ltd

Designs: Sarah Hatton
Photography: Heidi Coppock Beard
Styling: Sarah Hatton
Model: Opal Jocelyn Boss
Graphic Design: Darren Brant

ISBN 978-0-9567851-4-5

Printed in the United Kingdom

INTRODUCTION

Welcome to the fourth book in the Sarah Hatton Knits series. This time we have designed perfect, simple projects for precious little people and new arrivals.

I learnt to knit as a child and have always been passionate about fashion. After gaining my degree I was lucky enough to enter the world of handknit, professionally. I have been in the industry for over 10 years and have worked for brands including Rowan, Patons, Sirdar and Sublime. I love the hands-on approach that hand knit offers, it's also wonderful to be able to make gifts for loved ones as well as stylish garments for yourself.

I have taken my favourite winter yarns from the Rowan range and designed 10 simple projects. For each project you will find a list of equipment, how much yarn you will need and a clear, simple set of instructions free from the usual knitting jargon that can be terrifying for the beginner! Each pattern helps you learn a brand new technique, so before you know it you will have mastered knitting!

I hope you enjoy making the projects and don't forget to keep in touch via my website; www.sarahhatton.com

MOSS STITCH
HAT

MOSS STITCH HAT

FINISHED SIZE

Width

0-6	6-12	12-18	months
33	37	41	cm
13	14½	16	in

MATERIALS

YARN USED
Rowan All Seasons Cotton
1 x 50gm
(shown in Jersey 191, Iceberg 192 and Tornado 235)
YARN AMOUNTS ARE BASED ON AVERAGE
REQUIREMENTS AND ARE THEREFORE
APPROXIMATE

NEEDLES
1 pair 4½mm (US 7) needles

TENSION
19 stitches and 27 rows to 10cm/4in measured over
stocking stitch on 4½mm (US 7) needles.

INSTRUCTIONS

Using 4½mm needles cast on 63 [71:77] stitches.
Work 4 rows in stocking stitch (1 row knit, 1 row
purl).
Row 5: Knit 1, * purl 1, knit 1, repeat from * to end.
This row sets moss stitch.
Work 4 [5:6]cm/1½ [2:2½]in moss stitch, increase
1 [0:1] stitch at end of last row. 64 [71:78] stitches.
Continue in stocking stitch (1 row knit, 1 row purl)
until work measures 13 [14:17] cm/5 [5½:6½]in,
ending with right side facing for next row.
Shape crown
Next row: * Knit 5, knit 2 together, repeat from * to
last stitch, knit 1. 55 [61:67] stitches.
Work 1 row.
Next row: * Knit 4, knit 2 together, repeat from * to
last stitch, knit 1. 46 [51:56] stitches.
Work 1 row.
Next row: * Knit 3, knit 2 together, repeat from * to
last stitch, knit 1. 37 [41:45] stitches
Next row: Purl 1, * purl 2 together, purl 2, repeat
from * to end. 28 [31:34] stitches.
Next row: * Knit 1, knit 2 together, repeat from * to
last stitch, knit 1. 19 [21:23] stitches.
Next row: Purl 1, * purl 2 together, repeat from * to
end. 10 [11:12] stitches.
Break yarn and feed through remaining stitches.
Fasten off.

Using mattress stitch, join back seam.

GARTER STITCH
BLANKET

GARTER STITCH BLANKET

APPROX. FINISHED SIZE

47cm/18½in x 63cm/25in

MATERIALS

YARN USED
Rowan Baby Merino Silk DK
2 x 50gm each of Straw 671 and Clay 679
YARN AMOUNTS ARE BASED ON AVERAGE
REQUIREMENT AND ARE THEREFORE
APPROXIMATE

NEEDLES
1 pair 4mm (US 6) needles

TENSION
21 stitches and 41 rows to 10cm/4in measured
over garter stitch on 4mm (US 6) needles.

INSTRUCTIONS

Option 1 - Block method
Cast on 19 stitches.
Work in garter stitch (every row knit) for 9cm/3½in,
ending with right side row for next row.
Cast off.

Make 18 squares in shade A and 17 squares in
shade B.

MAKING UP
Using mattress stitch, join blocks together,
alternating them to create a chequerboard effect.

Option 2 -Worked in strips
Strip 1 (Make 3)
Using A cast on 19 stitches.
Working in garter stitch (every row knit) work
9cm/3½in, then work 9cm/3½in stripes in B, A, B,
A, B, A, ending each section with right side facing
for next row.
Cast off.

Strip 2 (Make 2)
Using B cast on 19 stitches.
Working in garter stitch (every row knit) work
9cm/3½in, then work 9cm/3½in stripes in A, B, A,
B, A, B, ending each section with right side facing
for next row.
Cast off.

MAKING UP
Using mattress stitch, join strips together,
alternating them to create a chequerboard effect.

GARTER STITCH

JACKET AND HAT

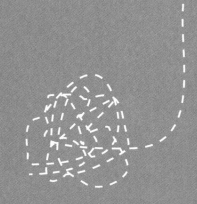

GARTER STITCH JACKET

FINISHED SIZE

To Fit

0-3   3-6   6-9   9-12   12-18 months

Actual Measurements (laid flat)
Width
25 [26:27:28:29]cm/10 [10¼:10½:11:11½]in
Length
21 [23:25:27:29]cm/8½ [9:10:10¾:11½]in
Sleeve length
12 [15:17:19:21]cm/4½ [6:6½:7½:8½]in

MATERIALS

YARN USED
Rowan Wool Cotton
Shade A – Frozen 977 1 [1:1:1:1] x 50gm
Shade B – Smalt 693 3 [3:3:3:4] x 50gm
YARN AMOUNTS ARE BASED ON AVERAGE
REQUIREMENT AND ARE THEREFORE
APPROXIMATE

NEEDLES
1 pair 4mm (US 6) needles

TENSION
21 stitches and 41 rows to 10cm/4in measured over
garter stitch on 4mm (US 6) needles.

INSTRUCTIONS

BACK
Using A cast on 53 [55:57:59:61] stitches.
Knit 16 [20:24:28:32] rows.
Change to B and continue in garter stitch until work
measures 21 [23:25:27:29]cm/8½ [9:10:10¾:11½]in,
ending with right side facing for next row.
Shape shoulders
Cast off 8 stitches at beginning of next 2 rows.
37 [39:41:43:45] stitches.
Cast off 8 [8:8:8:9] stitches at beginning of next 2
rows. 21 [23:25:27:27] stitches.
Cast off.

FOR A GIRL
LEFT FRONT
Using A cast on 31 [32:33:34:35] stitches.
Knit 16 [20:24:28:32] rows.
Change to B and cont in garter stitch until work
measures 15 [17:19:20:22]cm/6 [6½:7½:8:8¾]in,
ending with right side facing for next row.
Work 5 rows, ending with **wrong side** facing for next
row.
Shape front neck
Next row: Cast off 7 [8:9:10:10] stitches, knit to end.
24 [24:24:24:25] stitches.
Decrease 1 stitch at neck edge of next 5 [5:5:3:3]
rows, then on 3 [3:3:5:5] following alternate rows.
16 [16:16:16:17] stitches.
Continue without shaping until front matches back
to start of shoulder shaping, ending with right side
facing for next row.
Shape shoulder
Next row: Cast off 8 stitches, knit to end.
8 [8:8:8:9] stitches.
Work 1 row.
Cast off remaining stitches.

RIGHT FRONT
Using A cast on 31 [32:33:34:35] stitches.
Knit 16 [20:24:28:32] rows.
Change to B and cont in garter stitch until work
measures 15 [17:19:20:22]cm/6 [6½:7½:8:8¾]in,
ending with right side facing for next row.
Buttonhole row: Knit 2, knit 2 together, yarn forward,
knit to end.
Work 3 rows, ending with right side facing for next
row.
Shape front neck
Next row: Cast off 7 [8:9:10:10] stitches, knit to end.
24 [24:24:24:25] stitches.
Work 1 row.
Decrease 1 stitch at neck edge of next 5 [5:5:3:3]
rows, then on 3 [3:3:5:5] following alternate rows.
16 [16:16:16:17] stitches.
Continue without shaping until front matches back
to start of shoulder shaping, ending with right side
facing for next row.

Shape shoulder
Next row: Cast off 8 stitches, knit to end.
8 [8:8:8:9] stitches.
Work 1 row.
Cast off remaining stitches.

FOR A BOY
LEFT FRONT
Using A cast on 31 [32:33:34:35] stitches.
Knit 16 [20:24:28:32] rows.
Change to B and cont in garter stitch until work measures 15 [17:19:20:22]cm/6 [6½:7½:8:8¾]in, ending with right side facing for next row.
Work 1 row, ending with **wrong side** facing for next row.
Buttonhole row: Knit 2, knit 2 together, yarn forward, knit to end.
Work 3 rows, ending with **wrong side** facing for next row.

Shape front neck
Next row: Cast off 7 [8:9:10:10] stitches, knit to end.
24 [24:24:24:25] stitches.
Decrease 1 stitch at neck edge of next 5 [5:5:3:3] rows, then on 3 [3:3:5:5] following alternate rows.
16 [16:16:16:17] stitches.
Continue without shaping until front matches back to start of shoulder shaping, ending with right side facing for next row.

Shape shoulder
Next row: Cast off 8 stitches, knit to end.
8 [8:8:8:9] stitches.
Work 1 row.
Cast off remaining stitches.

RIGHT FRONT
Using A cast on 31 [32:33:34:35] stitches.
Knit 16 [20:24:28:32] rows.
Change to B and cont in garter stitch until work measures 15 [17:19:20:22]cm/6 [6½:7½:8:8¾]in, ending with right side facing for next row.
Work 4 rows, ending with right side facing for next row.

Shape front neck
Next row: Cast off 7 [8:9:10:10] stitches, knit to end.
24 [24:24:24:25] stitches.
Work 1 row.
Decrease 1 stitch at neck edge of next 5 [5:5:3:3] rows, then on 3 [3:3:4:4] following alternate rows. 16 [16:16:16:17] stitches.
Continue without shaping until front matches back to start of shoulder shaping, ending with right side facing for next row.

Shape shoulder
Next row: Cast off 8 stitches, knit to end.
8 [8:8:8:9] stitches.
Work 1 row.
Cast off remaining stitches.

SLEEVES
Using A cast on 29 [29:29:31:31] stitches.
Knit 15 [17:19:21:23] rows. (This will form turnback of sleeve).
Change to B and continue as follows:-
Work 14 [16:18:20:22] rows.
Next row: Knit into front and back of 1st st, knit to last 2 stitches, knit into front and back of next st, knit 1. 31 [31:31:33:33] stitches.
This row sets sleeve increasing.
Increase 1 stitch at each end of 4 [2:4:1:1] following 4th rows, then on 2 [5:5:8:9] following 6th rows.
43 [45:49:51:53] stitches.
Continue without shaping until sleeve measures 12 [15:17:19:21]cm/4½ [6:6½:7½:8½]in from end of turnback, ending with right side facing for next row.
Cast off 5 stitches at beginning of next 6 rows.
13 [15:19:21:23] stitches.
Cast off remaining stitches.

MAKING UP
Join both shoulder seams.
Collar
With right side facing and using B, starting 2cm/¾in in from front edge, pick up and knit 15 [16:17:20:20] stitches up right side of neck, 21 [23:25:27:27] stitches from back neck and 15 [16:17:20:20] stitches down left side of neck, ending 2cm/¾in in from front edge. 51 [55:59:67:67] stitches.
Knit 5 rows.
Next row: Knit 16 [18:20:21:21], (knit in to front and back of next stitch, knit 2) 6 [6:6:8:8] times, knit into front and back of next st, knit to end.
58 [62:66:76:76] stitches.
Continue in garter stitch until collar measures 5 [6:6:7:8]cm/2 [2½:2½:2¾:3]in, ending with wrong side facing for next row.
Cast off knitways.

MAKING UP
Place markers 10 [11:12:12:13]cm/4 [4¼:4½:4½:5] in, down side seam from shoulder. Join side seams to this marker. Join sleeve seams remembering to reverse the seam for turnback section. Sew in sleeves between markers. Sew on button.

GARTER STITCH HAT

FINISHED SIZE

Width

0-6	6-12	12-18	months
33	37	41	cm
13	14½	16	in

MATERIALS

YARN USED
Rowan Wool Cotton
Shade A – Smalt 693 1 x 50gm
Shade B – Frozen 977 1 x 50gm
YARN AMOUNTS ARE BASED ON AVERAGE
REQUIREMENT AND ARE THEREFORE
APPROXIMATE

NEEDLES
1 pair 4mm (US 6) needles

TENSION
21 stitches and 41 rows to 10cm/4in measured over
stocking stitch on 4mm (US 6) needles.

INSTRUCTIONS

Using 4mm needles and A cast on 69 [77:85]
stitches.
Work 16 [20:20] rows in garter stitch (every row knit)
to form turnback.
Change to B and continue in garter stitch until hat
measures 10 [11:14]cm/ 4 [4¼:5½]in, from end of
turnback, ending with right side facing for next row.
Shape crown
Next row: Knit 4, * knit 2 together, knit 6, repeat from
* to last stitch, knit 1. 61 [68:75] stitches.
Work 1 row.
Next row: Knit 4, * knit 2 together, knit 5, repeat from
* to last stitch, knit 1. 53 [59:65] stitches.
Work 1 row.
Next row: Knit 4, * knit 2 together, knit 4, repeat from
* to last stitch, knit 1. 45 [50:55] stitches.
Work 1 row.
Next row: Knit 4, * knit 2 together, knit 3, repeat from
* to last stitch, knit 1. 37 [41:45] stitches.
Work 1 row.

Next row: * Knit 2 together, knit 2, repeat from * to
last stitch, knit 1. 28 [31:34] stitches.
Next row: Knit 1, * knit 1, knit 2 together, repeat from
* to end. 19 [21:23] stitches.
Next row: * Knit 2 together, repeat from * to last
stitch, knit 1. 10 [11:12] stitches.
Break yarn and feed through remaining stitches.
Fasten off.

Using mattress stitch, join back seam, reversing
seam for the turnback section so that it does not
show in wear.

BLANKET WITH

SQUARES

BLANKET WITH SQUARES

APPROX. FINISHED SIZE

46cm/18in x 64cm/25in

MATERIALS

YARN USED
Rowan All Seasons Cotton
5 x 50gm (shown in Iceberg 192)
YARN AMOUNTS ARE BASED ON AVERAGE
REQUIREMENTS AND ARE THEREFORE
APPROXIMATE

NEEDLES
1 pair 4½mm (US 7) needles

TENSION
19 stitches and 27 rows to 10cm/4in measured over
stocking stitch on 4½mm (US 7) needle.

INSTRUCTIONS

Cast on 87 stitches.
Knit 8 rows.
Continue as follows:-
Row 1 and all following right side rows: Knit.
Row 2: Knit 4, purl to last 4 stitches, knit 4.
Row 4: Knit 4, purl 3, knit 21, purl 31, knit 21, purl
3, knit 4.
Rows 6 and 8: As row 4.
Row 10: Knit 4, purl 3, knit 3, purl 15, knit 3, purl 31,
knit 3, purl 15, knit 3, purl 3, knit 4.
Row 12: As row 10.
Row 14: Knit 4, purl 3, knit 3, purl 3, knit 9, purl 3,
knit 3, purl 31, knit 3, purl 3, knit 9, purl 3, knit 3, purl
3, knit 4.
Rows 16, 18, 20 and 22 : As row 14.
Rows 24 and 26: As row 10.
Rows 28, 30 and 32: As row 4.
Row 34: As row 2.
Row 36: Knit 4, purl 29, knit 21, purl 29, knit 4.
Rows 38 and 40: As row 36.
Row 42: Knit 4, purl 29, knit 3, purl 15, knit 3, purl
29, knit 4.
Row 44: As row 42.

Row 46: Knit 4, purl 29, knit 3, purl 3, knit 9, purl 3,
knit 3, purl 29, knit 4.
Rows 48, 50, 52 and 54: As row 46.
Rows 56 and 58: As row 42.
Rows 60, 62 and 64: As row 36.
(These 64 rows are also set out on the chart).
Repeat from row 1 to 64 once, then rows 1 to 34
once more.
Knit 9 rows.
Cast off knitways on the wrong side.

NOTE: CHART ON PAGE 44

PINAFORE

DRESS

PINAFORE DRESS

FINISHED SIZE

To Fit

| 0-3 | 3-6 | 6-9 | 9-12 | 12-18 | months |

Actual Measurements (laid flat)
Width
25 [26:27:28.5:29.5]cm/10 [10¼:10½:11:11½]in
Length
35 [37:40:42:44]cm/14 [14½:15½:16½:17½]in

MATERIALS

YARN USED
Rowan Baby Merino Silk DK
Shade A – Dawn 672 2 [3:3:3:4] x 50gm
Shade B – Zinc 681 1 x 50gm
YARN AMOUNTS ARE BASED ON AVERAGE
REQUIREMENT AND ARE THEREFORE
APPROXIMATE

4 buttons

NEEDLES
1 pair 3¼mm (US 3) needles
1 pair 4mm (US 6) needles

TENSION
22 stitches and 30 rows to 10cm/4in measured over
stocking stitch on 4mm (US 6) needles.

INSTRUCTIONS

BACK
Using 3¼mm needles and A cast on 69 [71:73:77:79]
stitches.
Knit 6 rows.
Change to 4mm needles.
Beginning with a knit row, work in stocking stitch
(1 row knit, 1 row purl) until work meas 22
[23:25:27:28]cm/8½ [9:10:10½:11]in, ending with a
knit row.
Shape yoke
Next row: Knit 6 [7:8:10:11], (knit 2 together, knit 3)
11 times, knit 2 together, knit 6 [7:8:10:11].

57 [59:61:65:67] stitches.
Change to 3¼mm needles.
Knit 1 row.
Using B, knit 2 rows.
Using A, knit 2 rows.
Repeat these 4 rows 3 times.
Working in A and garter stitch (every row knit)
continue as follows:-
Shape armholes
Cast off 3 [3:3:4:4] stitches at beginning of next
2 rows.
51 [53:55:57:59] stitches.
Next row: Knit 2, slip 1, knit 1, pass slipped stitch
over, knit to last 4 stitches, knit 2 together, knit 2.
Knit 1 row.
Repeat these 2 rows 3 times more.
43 [45:47:49:51] stitches. **
Continue without shaping until armhole measures
9 [10:11:11:12] cm/3½ [4:4¼:4¼:4½]in, ending with
right side facing for next row.
Shape back neck and shoulders
Next row: Knit 7 [7:8:8:9] stitches, knit 2 together,
knit 1, turn and continue on these 9 [9:10:10:11]
stitches only.
Next row: Knit.
Next row: Knit 6 [6:7:7:8], knit 2 together, knit 1.
8 [8:9:9:10] stitches.
Knit 9 rows.
Next row: Knit 1, knit 2 together, yarn forward, knit
1 [1:2:2:3], knit 2 together, yarn forward, knit 2.
Knit 4 rows.
Cast off knitways.
With right side facing, rejoin yarn to remaining
stitches, cast off 23 [25:25:27:27] stitches, (1 stitch
left on needle) , slip 1, knit 1, pass slipped stitch over,
knit to end. 9 [9:10:10:11] stitches.
Knit 1 row.
Next row: Slip 1, knit 1, pass slipped stitch over, knit
to end. 8 [8:9:9:10] stitches.
Knit 9 rows.
Next row: Knit 1, knit 2 together, yarn forward, knit 1
[1:2:2:3], knit 2 together, yarn forward, knit 2.
Knit 4 rows.
Cast off knitways.

FRONT

Work as given for Back to **.

Continue without shaping until armhole measures 4 [4:5:5:5]cm/1½ [1½:2:2:2]in, ending with right side facing for next row.

Shape front neck

Next row: Knit 13 [14:14:15:15], knit 2 together, knit 1, turn and continue on these 15 [16:16:17:17] stitches only.

Knit 1 row.

Next row: Knit 12 [13:13:14:14], knit 2 together, knit 1.

These 2 rows set neck shaping.

Decrease as set at neck edge of 2nd and 4 [4:3:4:3] following alternate rows, then on every following 4th row until 8 [8:9:9:10] stitches remain.

Continue without shaping until armhole measures 10 [11:12:12:13]cm/4 [4¼:4½:4½:5]in, ending with wrong side facing for next row.

Cast off knitways.

With right side facing, rejoin yarn to remaining stitches, cast off 11 [11:13:13:15] stitches, (1 stitch left on needle), slip 1, knit 1, pass slipped stitch over, knit to end.

Knit 1 row.

Next row: Knit 1, slip 1, knit 1, pass slipped stitch over, knit to end.

Decrease as set at neck edge of 2nd and 4 [4:3:4:3] following alternate rows, then on every following 4th row until 8 [8:9:9:10] stitches remain.

Continue without shaping until armhole measures 10 [11:12:12:13]cm/4 [4¼:4½:4½:5]in, ending with wrong side facing for next row.

Cast off knitways.

MAKING UP

Join side seams. Sew buttons to each front shoulder to match buttonholes on back.

ORIGAMI

BOOTIES

ORIGAMI BOOTIES

FINISHED SIZE

To fit an average sized babies foot for the following sizes

0-6   6-12   12-18   months

MATERIALS

YARN USED
1 x 50gm of either Rowan Wool Cotton or Rowan Baby Silk Merino DK
(shown for 6-12 mths in Wool Cotton Clear 941 and Frozen 977, Baby Silk Merino DK in Straw 671, Rose 678 and Dawn 672 with sole in Zinc 681)
YARN AMOUNTS ARE BASED ON AVERAGE REQUIREMENTS AND ARE THEREFORE APPROXIMATE

NEEDLES
1 pair 4mm (US 6) needles

INSTRUCTIONS

Shape sole
Cast on 6 [6:7] stitches.
Working in garter stitch (every row knit) increase 1 stitch at each end of 3rd and 2 following 4th row, then on following 6th row. 14 [14:15] stitches.
Work 13 [17:21] rows without shaping.
Decrease 1 stitch at each end of next and following 4th row. 10 [10:11] stitches.
Place a marker on the last row. (If you wish to make a bootee with a contrasting upper and lower you will need to change colour at this point.)
Shape upper
Continue in garter stitch on these 10 [10:11] stitches until strip fits from marker around sole, sewing in position at same time, using either blanket stitch for a visible seam or mattress stitch for an invisible seam.
Cast off and sew cast off edge in place under start of upper.
You will need to sew one shoe clockwise around the sole and one counter clockwise.
You may wish to work a small stitch where the two sides of the upper cross to help the bootee stay secure, alternatively you could secure using a decorative button ensuring it is attached very securely.

STRIPED JACKET AND HAT

STRIPED JACKET

FINISHED SIZE

To Fit

0-3   3-6   6-9   9-12   12-18 months

Actual Measurements (laid flat)
Width
25 [26:27:28:29]cm/10 [10¼:10½:11:11½]in
Length
24 [26:28:30:32]cm/9½ [10¼:11:12:12¾]in
Sleeve length
12 [15:17:19:21]cm/4½ [6:6½:7½:8½]in

MATERIALS

YARN USED
Rowan Baby Merino Silk DK
Shade A – Zinc 681 2 [2:2:3:3] x 50gm
Shade B – Dawn 672 1 [1:1:1:2] x 50gm
YARN AMOUNTS ARE BASED ON AVERAGE
REQUIREMENT AND ARE THEREFORE APPROXIMATE

4 buttons

NEEDLES
1 pair 3¼mm (US 3) needles
1 pair 4mm (US 6) needles

TENSION
22 stitches and 30 rows to 10cm/4in measured over
stocking stitch on 4mm (US 6) needles.

INSTRUCTIONS

BACK
Using 3¼mm needles and A cast on 54 [58:58:62:66]
stitches.
Row 1 (Right side): Knit 2, * purl 2, knit 2, repeat from
* to end.
Row 2: * Purl 2, knit 2, repeat from * to last 2 stitches,
purl 2.
These 2 rows set rib.
Work 5 [5:5:7:7] rows more in rib, ending with wrong
side facing for next row.
Next row: Rib to end and AT SAME TIME decrease
0 [1:0:0:1] stitch and increase 1 [0:1:0:0] stitch.
55 [57:59:62:65] stitches.
Change to 4mm needles and continue as follows:-

Row 1: Using B, knit.
Row 2: Using B, purl.
Repeat these 2 rows once more.
Row 5: Using A, knit.
Row 6: Using A, purl.
These 6 rows set stripe pattern.
Working in stripe pattern throughout, continue until work
meas 14 [15:16:18:19]cm/5½ [6:6¼:7:7½]in, ending with
right side facing for next row.
Shape armhole
Cast off 3 [3:3:3:4] stitches at beg of next 2 rows.
49 [51:53:56:57] stitches.
Next row: K2, slip 1, knit 1, pass slipped stitch over, knit
to last 4 stitches, knit 2 together, knit 2.
47 [49:51:54:55] stitches.
Work 1 row.
Repeat the last 2 rows 1 [1:1:2:2] times.
45 [47:49:50:51] stitches.
Continue without shaping until armhole measures 10
[11:12:12:13]cm/4 [4¼:4½:4½:5]in, ending with right
side facing for next row.
Shape shoulders
Cast off 5 stitches at beginning of next 2 rows.
35 [37:39:40:41] stitches.
Cast off 6 stitches at beginning of next 2 rows.
23 [25:27:28:29] stitches.
Cast off.

LEFT FRONT
Using 3¼mm needles and A cast on 23 [27:27:27:31]
stitches.
Row 1 (right side): Knit 2, * purl 2, knit 2, repeat from *
to last stitch, purl 1.
Row 2: Knit 1, * purl 2, knit 2, repeat from * to last 2
stitches, purl 2.
These 2 rows set rib.
Work 5 [5:5:7:7] rows more in rib.
Next row: Rib to end and AT SAME TIME decrease
0 [1:0:0:2] stitches and increase 2 [0:0:1:0] stitches
across row. 25 [26:27:28:29] stitches.
Change to 4mm needles and working in stripe pattern
as set on back continue until work matches back to
start of armhole shaping, ending with right side facing
for next row.
Shape armhole and front neck
Next row: Cast off 3 [3:3:3:4] stitches, knit to end.
22 [23:24:25:25] stitches.

Work 1 row.

Next row: K2, slip 1, knit 1, pass slipped stitch over, knit to last 4 stitches, knit 2 together, knit 2. 20 [21:22:23:23] stitches.

Work 1 row.

Repeat the last 2 rows 1 [1:1:2:2] times. 18 [19:20:19:19] stitches.

Next row: Knit to last 4 stitches, knit 2 together, knit 2.

This row sets neck decreasing.

Decrease as set at neck edge of 2nd and 1 [2:3:2:2] following alternate rows, then on every following 4th row until 11 stitches remain.

Continue without shaping until armhole matches back, ending with right side facing for next row.

Shape shoulder

Next row: Cast off 5 stitches, knit to end. 6 stitches.

Work 1 row.

Cast off remaining 6 stitches.

RIGHT FRONT

Using 3¼mm needles and A cast on 23 [27:27:27:31] stitches.

Row 1 (right side): Purl 1, * knit 2, purl 2, repeat from * to last 2 stitches, knit 2.

Row 2: Purl 2, * knit 2, purl 2, repeat from * to last stitch, knit 1.

These 2 rows set rib.

Work 5 [5:5:7:7] rows more in rib.

Next row: Rib to end and AT SAME TIME decrease 0 [1:0:0:2] stitches and increase 2 [0:0:1:0] stitches across row. 25 [26:27:28:29] stitches.

Change to 4mm needles and working in stripe pattern as set on back continue until work matches back to start of armhole shaping, ending with wrong side facing for next row.

Shape armhole and front neck

Next row: Cast off 3 [3:3:3:4] stitches, purl to end. 22 [23:24:25:25] stitches.

Next row: K2, slip 1, knit 1, pass slipped stitch over, knit to last 4 stitches, knit 2 together, knit 2. 20 [21:22:23:23] stitches.

Work 1 row.

Repeat the last 2 rows 1 [1:1:2:2] times. 18 [19:20:19:19] stitches.

Next row: Knit 2, slip 1, knit 1, pass slipped stitch over, knit to end.

This row sets neck decreasing.

Decrease as set at neck edge of 2nd and 1 [2:3:2:2] following alternate rows, then on every following 4th row until 11 stitches remain.

Continue without shaping until armhole matches back, ending with wrong side facing for next row.

Shape shoulder

Next row: Cast off 5 stitches, purl to end. 6 stitches.

Work 1 row.

Cast off remaining 6 stitches.

SLEEVES

Using 3¼mm needles and A cast on 30 [30:30:34:34] stitches.

Work 6 [6:6:8:8] rows in rib as set on back.

Change to 4mm needles and using A throughout continue as follows:-

Beginning with a K row and working in stocking stitch (1 row knit, 1 row purl) throughout, work 2 rows.

Next row: Knit into front and back of next st, knit to last 2 stitches, knit into front and back of next stitch, knit 1.

This row sets sleeve increases.

Increase as set at each end of 2nd [4th:2nd:4th:4th] and 1 [6:1:4:7] following 2nd [4th:2nd:4th:4th] row, then on 4 [0:7:3:2] following 4th [0:4th:6th:6th] rows. 44 [46:50:52:56] stitches.

Continue without shaping until sleeve measures 12 [15:17:19:21]cm/4½ [6:6½:7½:8½]in, ending with right side facing for next row.

Shape sleeve top

Cast off 3 [3:3:3:4] stitches at beginning of next 2 rows. 38 [40:44:46:48] stitches.

Next row: K2, slip 1, knit 1, pass slipped stitch over, knit to last 4 stitches, knit 2 together, knit 2. 36 [38:42:44:46] stitches.

Work 1 row.

Repeat the last 2 rows 1 [1:1:2:2] times. 34 [36:40:40:42] stitches.

Cast off 4 [4:5:5:5] stitches at beginning of next 6 rows. 10 [12:10:10:12] stitches.

Cast off remaining stitches.

MAKING UP

Join both shoulder seams.

Neckband

With RS facing, using 3¼mm needles and A pick up and knit 36 [39:41:47:49] stitches up right front edge to start of neck shaping, 26 [28:31:31:34] stitches up right side of neck, 24 [26:28:28:30] stitches from back neck, 26 [28:31:31:34] stitches down left side of neck and 36 [39:41:47:49] stitches down left front to cast on edge. 148 [160:172:184:196] stitches.

Row 1 (wrong side): Knit 1, purl 2, * knit 2, purl 2, repeat from * to last stitch, knit 1.

Row 2: Knit 1, * knit 2, purl 2, repeat from * to last 3 stitches, knit 3.

These 2 rows set rib.

Work 1 row more in rib.

For a boy
Next row: Rib to last 35 [38:41:44:47] stitches,
(rib 2 together, yarn forward, rib 8 [9:10:11:12] 3 times,
rib 2 together, yarn forward, rib 3.
For a girl
Next row: Rib 3, (rib 2 together, yarn forward,
rib 8 [9:10:11:12]) 3 times, rib 2 together, yarn forward,
rib to end.
For boy or girl
Next row: Rib to end, working into yarn forwards of last
row.
Work 4 rows more in rib.
Cast off in rib.

Join side and sleeve seams. Sew in sleeves. Sew on
buttons.

STRIPED HAT

FINISHED SIZE

To Fit	0-6	6-12	12-18	months
Width	33	37	41	cm

MATERIALS

YARN USED
Rowan Baby Merino Silk DK
1 x 50gm each of Zinc 681 and Dawn 672
YARN AMOUNTS ARE BASED ON AVERAGE
REQUIREMENTS AND ARE THEREFORE
APPROXIMATE

NEEDLES
1 pair 3.25mm (US 3) needles
1 pair 4mm (US 6) needles

TENSION
22 stitches and 30 rows to 10cm/4in measured over
stocking stitch on 4mm (US 6) needles.

INSTRUCTIONS

Using 4mm needles and A cast on 74 [82:90]
stitches.
Row 1 (right side): Knit 2, * purl 2, knit 2, repeat from
* to end.
Row 2: * Purl 2, knit 2, repeat from * to last 2 stitches,
purl 2.
These 2 rows set rib.
Work 8 rows more in rib.
Change to 4mm needles and continue as follows:-
Row 1(right side): Using B, knit.
Row 2: Using B, purl.
Repeat these 2 rows once more.
Row 5: Using A, knit.
Row 6: Using A, purl.
These 6 rows set stripe pattern.
Working in stripe pattern throughout, continue until
work measures 10 [13:16]cm/4 [5¼:6¼]in, ending
with right side facing for next row.
Shape crown
Next row: * Knit 6, knit 2 together, repeat from * to

last 2 stitches, knit 2. 65 [72:79] stitches.
Work 1 row.
Next row: * Knit 5, knit 2 together, repeat from * to
last 2 stitches, knit 2. 56 [62:68] stitches.
Work 1 row.
Next row: * Knit 4, knit 2 together, repeat from * to
last 2 stitches, knit 2. 47 [52:57] stitches.
Work 1 row.
Next row: * Knit 3, knit 2 together, repeat from * to
last 2 stitches, knit 2. 38 [42:46] stitches.
Work 1 row.
Next row: * Knit 2, knit 2 together, repeat from * to
last 2 stitches, knit 2. 29 [32:35] stitches.
Next row: Purl 2, * purl 2 together, purl 1, repeat from
* to end. 20 [22:24] stitches.
Next row: * Knit 2 together, repeat from * to end.
10 [11:12] stitches.
Break yarn and feed through remaining stitches.
Fasten off.

Using mattress stitch, join back seam.

FRILLY
CARDIGAN

FRILLY CARDIGAN

FINISHED SIZE

To Fit

| 0-3 | 3-6 | 6-9 | 9-12 | 12-18 | months |

Actual Measurements (laid flat)

Width	25 [26:27:28.5:29.5]cm/10 [10¼:10½:11:11½]in
Length	18 [20:22:24:26]cm/7 [8:8½:9½:10]in
Sleeve length	2cm/1in for all sizes

MATERIALS

YARN USED
Rowan Baby Merino Silk DK
2 [2:2:2:2] x 50gm (shown in Straw 671)
YARN AMOUNTS ARE BASED ON AVERAGE
REQUIREMENT AND ARE THEREFORE
APPROXIMATE

NEEDLES
1 pair 3¼mm (US 3) needles
1 pair 4mm (US 6) needles

TENSION
22 stitches and 30 rows to 10cm/4in measured over stocking stitch on 4mm (US 6) needles.

INSTRUCTIONS

BACK
Using 3¼mm needles and A cast on 165 [171:177:189:195] stitches.
Row 1 (Right side): * Knit 1, knit 2 together, repeat from * to end . 110 [114:118:126:130] stitches.
Row 2: * Purl 2 together, repeat from * to end. 55 [57:59:63:65] stitches.
Change to 4mm needles and beginning with a knit row and working in stocking stitch (1 row knit, 1 row purl) throughout continue until work measures 8 [9:10:12:13]cm/3 [3½:4:4¾:5]in, ending with right side facing for next row.

Shape armhole
Cast off 3 [3:3:3:4] stitches at beg of next 2 rows. 49 [51:53:57:57] stitches.
Next row: Knit 2, slip 1, knit 1, pass slipped stitch over, knit to last 4 stitches, knit 2 together, knit 2. 47 [49:51:55:55] stitches.
Work 1 row.
Repeat the last 2 rows 1 [1:1:2:2] times. 45 [47:49:51:51] stitches.
Continue without shaping until armhole measures 10 [11:12:12:13]cm/4 [4¼:4½:4½:5¼]in, ending with right side facing for next row.
Shape shoulders
Cast off 5 stitches at beginning of next 2 rows. 35 [37:39:41:41] stitches.
Cast off 6 stitches at beginning of next 2 rows. 23 [25:27:29:29] stitches.
Cast off remaining stitches.

LEFT FRONT
Using 3¼mm needles cast on 99 [102:105:111:114] stitches.
Row 1 (Right side): * Knit 1, knit 2 together, repeat from * to end . 66 [68:70:74:76] stitches.
Row 2: * Purl 2 together, repeat from * to end. 33 [34:35:37:38] stitches.
Change to 4mm needles and continue as follows:-
Row 1: Knit to last 5 stitches, knit 2 together, yarn forward, knit 3.
Row 2: Purl.
These 2 rows set front edge and stocking stitch.
Continue as set until left front matches back to start of armhole shaping, ending with right side facing for next row.
Shape armhole and front neck
Next row: Cast off 3 [3:3:3:4] stitches, knit to end. 30 [31:32:34:34] stitches.
Work 1 row.
Next row: Knit 2, slip 1, knit 1, pass slipped stitch over, knit to last 7 stitches, knit 2 together, pattern as set to end. 28 [29:30:32:32] stitches.
Work 1 row.
Repeat the last 2 rows 1 [1:1:2:2] times. 26 [27:28:28:28] stitches.
Next row: Knit to last 7 stitches, knit 2 together, pattern to end.
This row sets neck decreasing.

Decrease as set at neck edge of 2nd and every following alternate row until 17 stitches remain. Continue without shaping until armhole matches back, ending with right side facing for next row.

Shape shoulders

Next row: Cast off 5 stitches, pattern to end. 12 stitches.

Work 1 row.

Next row: Cast off 6 stitches, pattern to end. DO NOT BREAK OFF YARN and leave these stitches on a holder.

RIGHT FRONT

Using 3¼mm needles cast on 99 [102:105:111:114] stitches.

Row 1 (Right side): * Knit 1, knit 2 together, repeat from * to end . 66 [68:70:74:76] stitches.

Row 2: * Purl 2 together, repeat from * to end. 33 [34:35:37:38] stitches.

Change to 4mm needles and continue as follows:-

Row 1: Knit 3, yarn forward, slip 1, knit 1, pass slipped stitch over, knit to end.

Row 2: Purl.

These 2 rows set front edge and stocking stitch. Continue as set until left front matches back to start of armhole shaping, ending with right side facing for next row.

Shape armhole and front neck

Next row: Cast off 3 [3:3:3:4] stitches, purl to end. 30 [31:32:34:34] stitches.

Next row: Pattern 5 as set, slip 1, knit 1, pass slipped stitch over, knit to last 4 stitches, knit 2 together, knit 2. 28 [29:30:32:32] stitches.

Work 1 row.

Repeat the last 2 rows 1 [1:1:2:2] times. 26 [27:28:28:28] stitches.

Next row: Pattern 5 as set, slip 1, knit 1, pass slipped stitch over, knit to end.

This row sets neck decreasing.

Decrease as set at neck edge of 2nd and every following alternate row until 17 stitches remain. Continue without shaping until armhole matches back, ending with wrong side facing for next row.

Shape shoulders

Next row: Cast off 5 stitches, pattern to end. 12 stitches.

Work 1 row.

Next row: Cast off 6 stitches, pattern to end . DO NOT BREAK OFF YARN and leave these stitches on a holder.

SLEEVES

Using 3¼mm needles cast on 45 [49:53:55:59] stitches.

Row 1 (Right side): * Knit 1, purl 1, repeat from * to last stitch, knit 1.

Row 2: Purl 1, * knit 1, purl 1, repeat from * to end. Repeat these 2 rows once more.

Change to 4mm needles and beginning with a knit row, work 4 rows in stocking stitch (1 row knit, 1 row purl).

Shape sleeve top

Cast off 3 [3:3:3:4] stitches at beginning of next 2 rows. 39 [43:47:49:51] stitches.

Next row: K2, slip 1, knit 1, pass slipped stitch over, knit to last 4 stitches, knit 2 together, knit 2. 37 [41:45:47:49] stitches.

Purl 1 row.

Repeat the last 2 rows 1 [1:1:2:2] times. 35 [39:43:43:45] stitches.

Cast off 4 [4:5:5:5] stitches at beginning of next 6 rows. 11 [15:13:13:15] stitches.

Cast off remaining stitches.

MAKING UP

Join both shoulder seams.

Neckband

Working on 6 stitches left on a holder at each side of neck, continue in pattern until band fits across back neck to centre point, sewing in position at the same time. Cast off. Join cast off edges.

Join side and sleeves seams. Sew in sleeves. Sew as many buttons as you desire onto left front, using eyelets created in right front as buttonholes.

CHARTS

BLANKET WITH SQUARES

Legend:

knit
☐ RS: k nit stitch
WS: purl stitch

purl
● RS: purl stitch
WS: k nit stitch

OTHER INFORMATION

Tension

This is the size of your knitting. Most of the knitting patterns will have a tension quoted. This is how many stitches 10cm/4in in width and how many rows 10cm/4in in length to make a square. If your knitting doesn't match this then your finished garment will not measure the correct size. To obtain the correct measurements for your garment you must achieve the tension.

The tension quoted on a ball band is the manufacturer's average. For the manufacturer and designers to produce designs they have to use a tension for you to be able to obtain the measurements quoted. It's fine not to be the average, but you need to know if you meet the average or not. Then you can make the necessary adjustments to obtain the correct measurements.

How to make a Tension Square

First of all look at the tension details in your pattern. For example it might say "20stitches and 28 rows to 10cm/4in measured over stocking stitch using 4mm needles". Make sure you use the correct yarn and needles. Cast on at least 4 extra stitches than the tension states (this will give you the true width of all stitches) and work at least 4 extra rows.

Your knitting might be looser or tighter than the tension required, in which case you just need to alter your needle size. Go up one size if you have an extra stitch or two sizes if you have two extra stitches and the reverse if you have fewer stitches.

Choosing Yarn

Choosing yarn, as one of my friends once described "It is like shopping in an adult's sweetie shop". I think this sums it up very well. All the colours and textures, where do you start? Look for the thickness, how chunky do you want your finished garment? Sometimes it's colour that draws you to a yarn or perhaps you have a pattern that requires a specific yarn. Check the washing/care instructions before you buy.

Yarn varies in thickness; there are various descriptions such as DK and 4ply these are examples of standard weights. There are a lot of yarns available that are not standard and it helps to read the ball band to see what the recommended needle size is. This will give you an idea of the approximate thickness. It is best to use the yarn recommended in the pattern.

Keep one ball band from each project so that you have a record of what you have used and most importantly how to care for your garment after it has been completed. Always remember to give the ball band with the garment if it is a gift.

The ball band normally provides you with the average tension and recommended needle sizes for the yarn, this may vary from what has been used in the pattern, always go with the pattern as the designer may change needles to obtain a certain look. The ball band also tells you the name of the yarn and what it is made of, the weight and approximate length of the ball of yarn along with the shade and dye lot numbers. This is important as dye lots can vary, you need to buy your yarn with matching dye lots.

YARN AMOUNTS ARE BASED ON AVERAGE REQUIREMENT AND ARE THEREFORE APPROXIMATE

Pressing and Aftercare.

Having spent so long knitting your project it can be a great shame not to look after it properly. Some yarns are suitable for pressing once you have finished to improve the look of the fabric. To find out this information you will need to look on the yarn ball band, where there will be washing and care symbols.
Once you have checked to see if your yarn is suitable to be pressed and the knitting is a smooth texture (stocking stitch for example), pin out and place a damp cloth onto the knitted pieces. Hold the steam iron (at the correct temperature) approximately 10cm/4in away from the fabric and steam. Keep the knitted pieces pinned in place until cool.

As a test it is a good idea to wash your tension square in the way you would expect to wash your garment.

STOCKISTS

AUSTRALIA: Australian Country Spinners, Pty Ltd, Level 7, 409 St. Kilda Road, Melbourne Vic 3004.
Tel: 03 9380 3830
Email: sales@auspinners.com.au

AUSTRIA: Coats Harlander GmbH, Autokaderstrasse 31, A -1210 Wien. Tel: (01) 27716 – 0

BELGIUM: Coats Benelux, Ring Oost 14A, Ninove, 9400, Belgium Tel: 0346 35 37 00
Email: sales.coatsninove@coats.com

CANADA: Westminster Fibers Inc, 8 Shelter Drive, Greer South Carolina, NH03060 Tel: 800 445-9276
Email: rowan@westminsterfibers.com

CHINA: Coats Shanghai Ltd, No 9 Building ,
Baosheng Road, Songjiang Industrial Zone, Shanghai.
Tel: (86- 21) 5774 3733   Email: victor.li@coats.com

DENMARK: Coats Danmark A/S, Nannasgade 28, 2200 Kobenhavn N Tel: (45) 35 86 90 50
Fax: (45) 35 82 15 10 Email: info@hpgruppen.dk Web: www.hpgruppen.dk

FINLAND: Coats Opti Oy, Ketjutie 3, 04220 Kerava
Tel: (358) 9 274 871

FRANCE: Coats France / Steiner Frères, SAS 100, avenue du Général de Gaulle, 18 500 Mehun-Sur-Yèvre Tel: (33) 02 48 23 12 30
Web: www.coatscrafts.fr

GERMANY: Coats GmbH, Kaiserstrasse 1, D-79341 Kenzingen Tel: (49) 7644 8020
Web: www.coatsgmbh.de

HOLLAND: Coats Benelux, Ring Oost 14A, Ninove, 9400, Belgium Tel: 0346 35 37 00
Email: sales.coatsninove@coats.com

HONG KONG: Coats Shanghai Ltd, No 8 Building, Export & Processing Garden, Songjiang Industrial Zone, Shanghai.
Tel: (86- 21) 5774 3733-326
Email: victor.li@coats.com

ICELAND: Storkurinn, Laugavegi 59, 101 Reykjavik
Tel: (354) 551 8258 Email: storkurinn@simnet.is

ISRAEL: Beit Hasidkit, Sokolov St No2, 44256 Kfar Sava Tel: (972) 97482381

ITALY: Coats Cucirini s.r.l., Via Sarca 223, 20126 Milano Tel: 800 992377
Email: servizio.clienti@coats.com

KOREA: Coats Korea Co Ltd, 5F Eyeon B/D, 935-40 Bangbae- Dong, Seocho-Gu, Seoul Tel: (82) 2 521 6262.
Web: www.coatskorea.co.kr

LEBANON: y.knot, Saifi Village, Mkhalissiya Street 162, Beirut
Tel: (961) 1 992211 Email: y.knot@cyberia.net.lb

LUXEMBOURG: Bastel Kiste, Rue Du Fort Elizabeth 17-19, 1463 Luxemburg Tel: 00352 40 05 06

MALTA: John Gregory Ltd, 8 Ta'Xbiex Sea Front, Msida MSD 1512, Malta
Tel: +356 2133 0202, Email: raygreg@onvol.net

NEW ZEALAND: ACS New Zealand, 1 March Place, Belfast, Christchurch. Tel: 64-3-323-6665

NORWAY: Coats Knappehuset AS, Pb 100 Ulset, 5873 Bergen. Tel: (47) 55 53 93 00

SINGAPORE: Golden Dragon Store, 101 Upper Cross Street #02-51, People's Park Centre, Singapore 058357. Tel: (65) 6 5358454
Email: gdscraft@hotmail.com

SOUTH AFRICA: Arthur Bales LTD, 62 4th Avenue, Linden 2195 Tel: (27) 11 888 2401
Email: arthurb@new.co.za

SPAIN: Coats Fabra, Santa Adria 20, 08030 Barcelona Tel: 932908400
Email: atencion.clientes@coats.com

SWEDEN: Coats Expotex AB, Division Craft, JA Wettergrensgatta 7, Vastra Frolunda, 431 30 Goteburg Goteborg Tel: (46) 33 720 79 00

SWITZERLAND: Coats Stroppel AG, CH -5300 Turgi (AG) Tel: (41) 562981220

TAIWAN: Cactus Quality Co Ltd, 7FL-2, No 140, Roosevelt Road, Sec 2,Taipei, Taiwan, R.O.C.
Tel: 886-2-23656527 Email: cqcl@m17.hinet.net

THAILAND: Global Wide Trading, 10 Lad Prao Soi 88, Bangkok 10310. Tel: 00 662 933 9019
Email: global.wide@yahoo.com

U.S.A: Westminster Fibers Inc, 8 Shelter Drive, Greer South Carolina, NH03060.
Tel: 800 445-9276
Email: rowan@westminsterfibers.com

U.K: Rowan, Green Lane Mill, Holmfirth,
West Yorkshire, England HD9 2DX.
Tel: +44 (0) 1484 681881 Fax: +44 (0) 1484 687920
Email: mail@knitrowan.com
Web: www.knitrowan.com

ACKNOWLEDGEMENTS

Many thanks to Heidi for her beautiful photography.
Jeff and Emma for all their help and of course Opal
for being a bundle of joy!

To Darren for making the book look great and to all
my friends and family for their support.

Kate Buller and all at Rowan for their support.
Sharon Brant for her endless help and support
since becoming a freelance designer - thank you for
persuading me to take the jump!